SUMMER PASTA COOKBOOK

10 Classic Italian Recipes from the
PIATTO Cooking Channels

PIATTO RECIPES
in collaboration with PIATTO

Copyright © 2022 PIATTO LLC

All rights reserved

No part of this book may be reproduced, or stored in a retrieval system, or transmitted in any form or by any means, electronic, mechanical, photocopying, recording, or otherwise, without express written permission of the publisher.

You can find our video recipes at: youtube.com/piattorecipes
Our website: piattorecipes.com

Cover design by: PIATTO LLC

CONTENTS

Title Page
Copyright
Foreword
PASTA BASICS — 3
Creamy Garlic and Olive Oil Spaghetti — 7
Fresh 'Caprese' Penne with Tomato, Mozzarella & Basil — 12
Spaghetti with Clams — 17
Fettuccine Alfredo — 22
Vineyard Vegetable Pasta — 27
Garden Pasta — 33
Pesto Pasta with Green Beans and Potatoes — 37
Nerano Spaghetti — 42
Spaghetti with Mussels and Tomatoes — 47
Spaghetti Cacio and Pepe — 52
About The Author — 59

MORE PASTA?

youtube.com/PIATTORECIPES

FOREWORD

In this cookbook, we celebrate summer pasta! You'll discover traditional Italian pasta recipes that are perfect for summer—no oven required!

The mission of PIATTO™ and PIATTO Recipes™ Cooking Channels is to make cooking traditional Italian food easy! Our tested recipes, mouthwatering photography and step-by-step video recipes will help you master your favorite dishes.

This book is fully illustrated, so you'll never have to wonder what the final dish is supposed to look like. To supplement the recipes in this cookbook, we've included links to any video recipes available.

In fact, we invite you to subscribe to our cooking channel —youtube.com/piattorecipes—to see what other mouthwatering recipes we're cooking up!

Are These Recipes Authentic?

Whenever possible, we always try to identify the 'official' or most typical and popular version of the recipes that we share with you. The pasta recipes in this cookbook come from all over Italy. That means you'll discover many delicious recipes you've never encountered in your favorite Italian restaurant abroad.

The PIATTO™ creators and contributors are ambassadors of Italian cuisine who have grown up and lived in Italy. Unlike many cookbooks and restaurants abroad, we know what is considered traditional in Italy. We can't wait to share these mouthwatering classics with you and your family.

Happy cooking and... buon appetito!

SUMMER PASTA COOKBOOK

PASTA BASICS

How To Salt Pasta

Italian pasta is almost always salted while it is cooking to maximize its flavor. However, there are exceptions to this rule, which we'll explain in a minute. If your pasta dish does *not* include seafood broth or a large quantity of salty cheese, this is the rule of thumb:

Add about 1 tbsp (10 grams) of coarse salt for every 4 cups of water (about a 1 liter).

Use 4 cups (1 liter) of water for every portion of pasta that you are cooking—that's about 3.5 oz (100 g) of pasta.

The water is usually salted when the pasta is already cooking, about halfway through the cooking time. When making pasta for four people, about 2 handfuls of coarse salt is usually enough.

Italians typically use coarse salt (*sale grosso*) for salting pasta. It's easy to manage and produces a consistent result.

When Not To Salt The Water

If you are making a pasta dish that includes other very salty ingredients, you should *not* salt the pasta as it cooks. Alternatively, you'll want to reduce the salt you add by half. Then, you will taste and add salt as needed in the final dish.

For instance, this is the case with many seafood pasta dishes. Whether you are making your own seafood broth by steaming shellfish or buying pre-prepared seafood broth, seafood broth is very salty. It contains water from the salty ocean which the shellfish have expelled to produce that flavorful broth.

Similarly, some cheeses are very salty—such as pecorino, salted ricotta and Parmigiano Reggiano. If your pasta dish contains a large amount of these cheeses, you'll want to skip salting the pasta water or do so with caution.

How To Cook Pasta

Unless our recipe specifies otherwise, use these guidelines when cooking pasta for dishes in this cookbook!

To cook pasta, bring the water to a gentle boil. Then, add the pasta to the boiling water. Stir occasionally in the beginning to keep the pasta from sticking together. Salt (as we just discussed) is typically added halfway through the cooking time.

Different pasta requires different cooking times—anywhere from 2 to 20 minutes. Cooking time depends on factors like the size and shape of the pasta, as well as the ingredients used to make the pasta.

Also, fresh pasta always requires less cooking time than the same pasta dried. Why? The fresh pasta already has more water. Dry pasta is dry because it lost water during the drying process and needs time to reabsorb that water as it cooks. Fresh pasta often cooks very fast: 2-3 minutes is usually enough!

In Italy, pasta is almost always cooked just until it reaches an *al dente* consistency. 'Al dente' literally means 'to the teeth' in Italian. This means that the pasta is still a touch firm when bitten.

There is one situation when you won't cook the pasta in boiling water until it is *al dente*. For some pasta dishes, you need to finish cooking the pasta in a pan with a sauce or a flavorful broth. In this case, the recipe may call for cooking the pasta in the pot for just *part* of the cooking time. After that, you'll transfer the partially cooked pasta to a skillet to finish cooking it to the *al dente* stage.

Now, we've finished with the basics. Let's start cooking!

◆ ◆ ◆

PIATTO RECIPES

CREAMY GARLIC AND OLIVE OIL SPAGHETTI

"Spaghetti Aglio e Olio e Peperoncino"

PREP TIME: 5 MINUTES **COOKING TIME:** 11 MINUTES | **SERVES:** 4

The fastest pasta dish in Italy! This simple pasta dish is nonetheless packed with flavor. It is a favorite in Italy for lunch breaks or for a midnight snack. Spaghetti Aglio e Olio is popular throughout Italy, but originated in Naples.

It evolved as a 'poor man's' version of Spaghetti with Clam Sauce. Essentially, it's the same pasta dish but without the clams! In fact, in Neapolitan dialect, this dish is often referred to as 'Vermicelli con le Vongole Fujute' which literally means 'pasta in which the clams escaped' in Italian.

Some common variations? Add anchovies, toasted

breadcrumbs or chili pepper—as we're doing here.

◆ ◆ ◆

INGREDIENTS

fresh red chili pepper: 4, minced
fresh garlic: 4 cloves
olive oil: 12 tbsp (3/4 cup)
parsley: a handful
fine salt: to taste
pasta: 14 oz (400 g); spaghetti, vermicelli or linguine

◆ ◆ ◆

STEP-BY-STEP

Or, watch the video recipe on our YouTube Cooking Channel!

Partially Cook The Pasta

Bring a pot of water to a boil. Do *not* add salt to the water. We will be adding ladles of this hot water to a skillet to finish cooking the spaghetti. If you add salty water to cook the pasta, the water will evaporate in the skillet leaving too much salt in our dish. Yuck!

Prepare The Ingredients

Thinly slice the cloves of fresh garlic. After removing the seeds, mince the red chili peppers. Mince a handful of parsley and set it aside. Save the parsley stems for flavoring the oil!

Cook The Pasta

When the water is boiling, cook the pasta for just 2 minutes. In the meantime...

Make The Soffritto

Cover the bottom of a large skillet with the olive oil. Over medium heat, add the garlic, chili pepper and some parsley stems. Cook for about 2 minutes or until the garlic has turned golden. Sautéing aromatics in oil to create a base for a sauce or dish is called making a *soffritto* in Italian.

When the pasta has cooked for 2 minutes...

Finish Cooking The Pasta In The Pan

Transfer the spaghetti immediately to the infused olive oil along with 2 ladles of hot pasta water. Save the hot pasta water—we will continue adding it to the skillet to cook the pasta!

Now, we cook the pasta like a risotto over medium heat. Set your timer for the rest of the cooking time required on the pasta package instructions for *al dente* pasta. Total cooking time for the average spaghetti brand is about 11 minutes. In this case, you'd set your timer for 9 minutes since we already cooked the pasta for 2 minutes.

When the first ladles of pasta water have been mostly absorbed, add a few ladles more. Continue adding water a few ladles at a time until the pasta is cooked to *al dente*.

You should see a creamy sauce forming from the water and the oil because the pasta is releasing its starch directly into the sauce as it cooks. This creates an emulsion between the water and oil, producing a creamy sauce.

When the pasta is cooked, salt to taste and add some minced parsley for freshness and color. Buon appetito!

WATCH IT

Or, watch the video recipe on our YouTube Cooking Channel!

TIPS

Garlic digestion problems?
If garlic has a tendency to bother your digestion, add halved pieces of garlic to the olive oil instead of sliced or minced garlic. Then, discard the pieces of garlic after it has infused the olive oil. You can do the same with the chili pepper.

Chili Pepper Selection
We typically use red 'thai' chili peppers ('rawit' or 'birds eye') for this dish. Obviously, use chili pepper to suit your taste. Or, you can leave it out entirely since chili pepper is technically a variation.

Pasta Selection
For the creamiest sauce, choose a pasta that will release a lot of starch while cooking. Look for pasta that says it is 'bronze drawn' (*trafilato al bronzo*). This means that the pasta is cut with a bronze pasta stamp or cutter, which creates a more porous texture. This texture has many advantages, including allowing the pasta to release more starch!

Tasty Variations: Breadcrumbs or Anchovies
For a nice crunch, you can toast breadcrumbs with a tablespoon of extra virgin olive oil and sprinkle that on top of the pasta before serving it.

You can also melt a couple of anchovy filets together with the garlic to add extra flavor.

SUMMER PASTA COOKBOOK

FRESH 'CAPRESE' PENNE WITH TOMATO, MOZZARELLA & BASIL

"Pasta con Pomodori Freschi, Mozzarella e Basilico"

PREP TIME: 15 MINUTES **COOKING TIME:** 10 MINUTES | **SERVES:** 4

A summertime favorite! This fast and fresh dish includes all of the ingredients of a 'caprese' salad. It is a quintessential example of a Mediterranean diet recipe. Further, using unheated olive oil—as we do here—is the best way to maximize its many health benefits.

The tomato season in Italy begins by late spring and lasts all summer long. Italians take full advantage of it by making tomato sauces with fresh tomatoes, barely cooked to preserve their natural flavor. The addition of

Parmigiano Reggiano cheese and extra virgin olive oil makes this dish both delicious and nutritious. To top it off, we've added fresh mozzarella (fior di latte) at the end of the cooking. This pasta recipe is fast, easy and perfect for a hot day.

◆ ◆ ◆

INGREDIENTS

mozzarella: 1/4 pound (125 g); fresh or water-packed
Parmigiano Reggiano: 3 tbsp; grated
fresh tomatoes: 1 pound (500 g); beefsteak or Roma
fine salt: to taste
fresh garlic: 2 cloves
olive oil: 4 tablespoon
black pepper: 1/4 tsp
basil: several leaves
penne or rigatoni: 11 oz (320 g)

◆ ◆ ◆

STEP-BY-STEP

Or, watch the video recipe on our YouTube Cooking Channel!

Prepare The Cheese

Slice the mozzarella, then dice it into bite-size pieces. Measure out the Parmigiano Reggiano. Grate the cheese fresh from a wedge if possible for maximum flavor. Set the cheeses aside.

Prepare The Tomato Sauce

Make a shallow 'X' cut on one side of each tomato. Add the

tomatoes to a large pot of boiling water. Boil the tomatoes for a little over a minute. Save the hot water for cooking the pasta.

Peel the tomatoes. Then roughly mash the tomatoes into a pulp using a ricer, a fork or immersion blender. Strain the watery liquid from the tomatoes and keep the pulp.

Add a pinch of salt to the mashed tomatoes. Let the tomatoes rest for 5 minutes. The salt will extract more water from the tomatoes. Then use a spoon to remove and discard any watery liquid from the mashed tomatoes.

Add to the tomatoes: fresh garlic, fresh basil, Parmigiano cheese, extra virgin olive oil and black pepper. Mix to combine.

Let the tomato sauce rest for at least 10 minutes to develop the flavors. The longer you let it rest, the more flavorful the sauce will be. You can even prepare the sauce the night before for maximum flavor!

Finish With Pasta

Cook the pasta according to the package instructions. You can use the water in which you boiled the fresh tomatoes to cook the pasta.

In a large bowl, combine the drained pasta, the mozzarella and the fresh tomato sauce. Mix. Drizzle on more extra-virgin olive oil. Add a few more leaves of fresh basil and serve!

WATCH IT

Or, watch the video recipe on our YouTube Cooking Channel!

◆ ◆ ◆

TIPS

Use Fresh Mozzarella

For a dish like this, Italians use fresh, water-packed mozzarella called 'fior di latte' (which means 'the flower of milk'). Another possible alternative is the buffalo mozzarella.

Use Real Parmigiano

Always choose 'Parmigiano Reggiano' cheese—not 'parmesan'. For maximum flavor, buy a wedge of cheese (aged at least 24 months) and freshly grate the cheese.

Tomato Matters

Fresh tomatoes are the main ingredient here. Choose ripe tomatoes that have a lot of pulp, such as beefsteak tomatoes. Roma are a good choice as well.

◆ ◆ ◆

PIATTO RECIPES

SPAGHETTI WITH CLAMS

"Spaghetti alle Vongole"

PREP TIME: 2.5 HOURS **COOKING TIME:**
30 MINUTES | **SERVES:** 4

An extremely popular seafood dish in Italy, this recipe is often served for Christmas Eve or New Year's. However, it is also quite popular in the summertime—anytime the seafood is fresh!

We'll explain how to achieve a perfect, creamy seafood sauce without any additional ingredients—just like the best chefs make this dish in Italy!

◆ ◆ ◆

INGREDIENTS

clams: 2.2 pounds (1 kg)
fresh garlic: 3 cloves (one whole and 2 minced)

italian flat leaf parsley: 2 handfuls, roughly chopped
white wine: 1/2 cup (100 ml)
red chili pepper: 1/2 a fresh pepper
olive oil: as needed
salt and pepper: to taste
coarse salt: for pasta
spaghetti: 11 oz (320 g)

◆ ◆ ◆

STEP-BY-STEP

Or, watch the video recipe on our YouTube Cooking Channel!

Discard Unhealthy Clams

Give each clam a tap on a work surface. Those that remain closed (or close after you tap them) are likely healthy. Discard any clams that have broken shells or whose shells open when tapped.

Soak The Clams

Clams tend to contain a lot of sand. For this reason, they are usually soaked before cooking with them. During the soak, the clams will exchange the sandy water in their shells for the fresh salty water you provide them.

Prepare a salt water solution for soaking the clams. To do this, add 2 tablespoons (35 g) of fine salt to 4 cups (1 liter) of water.

Soak the healthy clams in the salted water for at least 2 hours.

Then, remove the clams from the soaking water using a slotted spoon. Don't just strain the water and clams as you would do when straining pasta. Why? We don't want to stir up any sand that came out during the soak and has settled in the bottom of the bowl. Discard the water that the clams have soaked in.

TIP: Don't be surprised when the clams poke their heads out during the soak. This is totally normal! Remember, the clams are still alive. They are opening up to replace the (sandy) salt water in their shells with the fresh salt water you've provided them.

Steam The Clams

Cover the bottom of a large pan or skillet with olive oil. Bring to medium heat. Then add a handful of roughly chopped parsley and one whole clove of garlic.

Sauté the parsley and garlic for about 30 seconds, then add the clams and stir.

Add 1/2 cup (100 ml) of white wine. Then cover the pan and steam the clams over medium heat until most of the clam shells have opened. Discard any clams that remain unopened after steaming.

Leave a handful of clams in their shells for decorating the finished pasta. Remove the meat from the rest of the clams.

Strain all of the clam broth produced to remove any residual sand. Add the strained broth to the clam meat to prevent it from drying out. Set the clams aside.

Cook The Pasta

Add the spaghetti to boiling water and cook for *half* of the time recommended on the package for *al dente* pasta. Do *not* add salt to the water. In the meantime...

Make A Soffritto

Mince two cloves of garlic and a handful of fresh parsley. Cover the bottom of a large pan or skillet with olive oil. Bring to medium heat. Then add the chili pepper, minced garlic and parsley to the hot oil. Sauté briefly to infuse the oil with flavor.

Add all of the clams and the strained clam broth to the same skillet.

Finish With Pasta

When the spaghetti is halfway cooked, transfer it immediately to the skillet with the clams—saving the hot pasta water! Add 2 ladles of hot pasta water and give it a stir. Finish cooking the pasta in the clam sauce—uncovered—over medium heat. Cook the pasta until it is *al dente*.

The sauce will thicken naturally due to the starch released by the spaghetti as it cooks. When the pasta is almost ready, add the clams in the shell to the skillet as well to warm them.

Top the finished pasta with minced fresh parsley and serve!

WATCH IT

Or, watch the video recipe on our YouTube Cooking Channel!

◆ ◆ ◆

TIPS

Selecting Clams

Use 'vongole veraci' when you can find them. Clam varieties differ in taste and are reflected in their price!

Preventing Sand in Your Clam Sauce

Sandy bites will absolutely ruin this dish! For this reason, pay special attention to the section on prepping the clams. We only want to use healthy clams and of course we want to avoid any sand in our final sauce. Clams are notorious for containing a lot of sand in their shells, and so the pre-soak is important for helping to remove that excess sand before steaming them.

◆ ◆ ◆

SUMMER PASTA COOKBOOK

FETTUCCINE ALFREDO

"Fettuccine Burro e Parmigiano"

PREP TIME: 10 MINUTES **COOKING TIME:** 10 MINUTES | **SERVES:** 4

Probably one of the most iconic dishes associated with Italy abroad, Fettuccine Alfredo is also one of the easiest and tastiest pasta recipes you can make at home.

The irony? If you ask for Fettuccine Alfredo outside of tourist areas in Italy, most Italians will look at you perplexed. They might ask who this 'Alfredo' is and why he has a pasta dish named after him! Italians know this dish by a name that translates to 'fettuccine (or pasta) butter and parmigiano.' This simple dish dates back to the 1400s.

The 'Alfredo' in 'Fettuccine Alfredo' refers to Alfredo di Lelio, the owner of a restaurant in Rome who began serving this common Italian dish in the 1900s under the name "fettuccine al triplo burro" (fettuccine with tripled butter).

The dish was famous then (as it is now) for its creamy

sauce, but also because it was finished at the table in a theatrical manner. The pasta quickly became a favorite of tourists who loved how the restaurant prepared the dish with flair and they began calling it Fettuccine Alfredo.

The butter to cheese ratio makes this an easy dish for beginners to prepare. This is because the cheese easily melts in the butter, creating a creamy and rich sauce that is desired around the world. There is no need to add heavy cream to this dish, and it's not traditional to do so.

◆ ◆ ◆

INGREDIENTS

butter: 6.5 tbsp (90 g)
Parmigiano Reggiano: 6 oz (180 g); finely grated
fettuccine: 11 oz (320 g) if dry fettuccine is used or 1 pound of fresh fettuccine

◆ ◆ ◆

STEP-BY-STEP

Or, watch the video recipe on our YouTube Cooking Channel!

Prepare The Ingredients

Finely grate the Parmigiano Reggiano cheese. Once grated, sift the cheese as well. It must have a powdery consistency for this recipe in order to melt evenly. Alternatively, you can buy finely grated Parmigiano.

Cut the butter into small cubes.

Cook The Pasta

Cook the fettuccine in gently boiling water. A gently boiling water will help you to avoid breaking this thin egg pasta, which tends to be more delicate than something like spaghetti. Salt the pasta water less than you normally would, since Parmigiano cheese is quite salty.

If you are using fresh pasta, it will only take 2-3 minutes to cook the pasta. Otherwise, follow the package instructions.

Finish With Pasta

Drain the pasta but do not discard the pasta water!

On a large serving dish or bowl, add half of the butter. Then, add the hot drained pasta on top of the butter. Top the pasta with the rest of the butter.

Using a spoon and a fork, mix the pasta and butter delicately until the butter is melted and coats the pasta.

Then add the Parmigiano Reggiano cheese, a couple of spoons at a time. Continue to mix, distributing the cheese throughout the pasta.

Add a ladle of hot pasta water and mix again. The creamy sauce will start to form. Continue adding more cheese (and more hot water if needed) until you have created a thin white sauce.

Buon appetito!

NOTE: The sauce will continue to thicken on the plate as the butter cools.

WATCH IT

Or, watch the video recipe on our YouTube Cooking Channel!

◆ ◆ ◆

TIPS

Use Real Parmigiano

Always, always use real Parmigiano Reggiano cheese for this dish. It is also important to select a Parmigiano that is aged a minimum of 24 months, though 36 months of aging is even better!

In a hurry?

Feel free to buy finely grated Parmigiano in the store if you don't want to take the time to freshly grate the cheese. It won't be quite as flavorful, but the cheese should be the right consistency for making a creamy sauce.

Heavy Cream? No way!

Do not use heavy cream. It only adds calories, not flavor. Cream won't make it any easier to create that beautiful, creamy sauce that you crave.

Heavy cream is likely used in restaurants and commercial sauces because butter is solid at room temperature. So, to sell a pre-prepared sauce, cream is added. You don't need it here.

Chicken or Veggies? Not Traditional

One of the hallmarks of Italian cuisine is that it tends to follow a 'less is more' philosophy. Italians love the simplicity of a dish with just a few, quality ingredients in the perfect proportion. This dish is the perfect example!

◆ ◆ ◆

PIATTO RECIPES

VINEYARD VEGETABLE PASTA

"Pasta Vignarola Romana"

PREP TIME: 20 MINUTES **COOKING TIME:** 30 MINUTES | **SERVES:** 4-5

This creamy pecorino cheese pasta is inspired by the classic Roman dish called 'Vignarola Romana'—a mix of vegetables that includes peas, artichokes, spring onions, fava (broad beans), lettuce and mint. The dish is named 'vignarola' (or 'vineyard') because all of the vegetables in it were traditionally grown between the grapevine rows.

While there is no one traditional recipe for pasta Vignarola, we think this one is absolutely delicious. In fact, fresh fava (broad beans) and pecorino romano cheese are a classic Italian combination! So, why not combine a pecorino-based Cacio e Pepe sauce with all of those healthy and tasty vegetables?

INGREDIENTS

VIGNAROLA
fava beans (broad beans): 1/2 pound (250 g)
peas: 4 oz (120 g)
artichoke hearts: about 6, quartered; fresh or from a can
romaine lettuce: several leaves (75 g)
spring onions: 2; sliced
fresh mint: 4 leaves
extra-virgin olive oil: 4-6 tbsp
salt and pepper: to taste

PASTA
'vignarola' mixed vegetables: 5 tbsp from mix above (serve the rest as a side)
pecorino romano cheese: 7 oz (200 g); finely grated
black pepper: 1/2 tbsp
pasta: 11 oz (320 g); choose 'tube' pasta like penne, rigatoni or paccheri

STEP-BY-STEP

Or, watch the video recipe on our YouTube Cooking Channel!

Make The Mixed Vegetables (Vignarola)

Generously cover the bottom of a large pan with olive oil. Bring to medium heat. Add the thinly sliced spring onions to the pan and cook them until they are tender.

Add the quartered artichoke hearts to the pan with a 1/2 cup of water. Cook covered for 5 minutes.

Add the fava (broad beans) and peas to the pan with another 1/4 cup of water. Cook covered for 15 minutes.

During the 15 minutes, check periodically to see if the vegetables have reached the level of tenderness that you prefer.

When the rest of the vegetables are cooked to your liking, add bite-size pieces of the lettuce. Give it a quick stir and cook the vegetables for about a minute longer.

Finally, add the mint! Let the mint infuse the vegetables for at least a minute. Set aside about 5 tablespoons of the finished mixed vegetables to add to the pasta (below). Serve the rest of the mixed vegetables as a side dish!

Toast The Black Pepper

Add freshly ground black pepper to a dry skillet over low heat. Toast the pepper very briefly—just until you start to smell it. Then quickly remove the pepper from heat.

Start Boiling The Pasta

Add the pasta to a pot of boiling water. Use less water than you normally would to boil the pasta. This will create a pasta water richer in starch, which we will then use to make our sauce!

Cook the pasta for 3/4 of the time recommended in the package instructions for *al dente* pasta. We'll finish cooking the pasta in the pan. In the meantime...

Create The Pecorino Paste

Combine the finely grated pecorino cheese with some hot pasta water from the boiling pasta. Add a ladle of the pasta water slowly to the cheese, mixing vigorously. Mix the water and cheese thoroughly until you have created a smooth pasta. The finished paste will look a bit like ricotta cheese. Then, set the cheese paste aside.

Technically, the water you add to the pecorino cheese should never be hotter than 140°F (60°C). If the water is any hotter, we risk creating clumpy, stringy cheese. However, by drizzling the hot pasta water in slowly and mixing continuously, you can typically avoid using a thermometer.

Add Pasta Water To The Pepper

Add a few ladles of hot pasta water to the toasted pepper in the pan. Simmer over medium heat for a few minutes to infuse the water with the black pepper.

Finish Cooking The Pasta In Pepper Water

When the pasta has cooked 3/4 of the way, transfer it to the skillet with the infused pepper water. Add 2 more ladles of pasta water and finish cooking the pasta to *al dente*.

Add the mixed vegetables (*vignarola*) that you previously set aside for the pasta. Stir to combine the vegetables with the pasta.

Add The Pecorino Paste

Remove the pan from the heat. Add the pecorino paste and mix quickly to combine it with the hot pasta until it is coats the pasta evenly.

Serve immediately!

WATCH IT

Or, watch the video recipe on our YouTube Cooking Channel!

◆ ◆ ◆

TIPS

Choose Tube Pasta
We like a tube pasta for this dish: rigatoni, penne, paccheri or similar. Why? The delicious cheese sauce and the veggies can

nestle inside those little holes, which is super tasty!

Or… Serve as a Side!

As we mentioned, the 'vignarola' can be served alone as an appetizer, a side dish or even a main dish. With this recipe, you essentially get two dishes in one!

Remove the skin of the fava? You decide!

Fresh fava beans need to be removed from their shells. You can also remove the outer *skin* of the beans of you like, but it's not necessary. You decide, based on your taste!

Want tender veggies? Cook the Vignarola longer.

Although we don't recommend overcooking the vegetables, you may decide to cook them longer than we've recommended if you prefer that these vegetables be more tender. Note that you will lose some flavor and color as you extend the cooking time.

Selecting Pecorino Cheese

There are many types of pecorino cheese and they are all good in this sauce! In fact, most regions in Italy have a pecorino cheese bearing their name—and all have a slightly unique taste.

Pecorino Romano (less aged or 'semi stagionato') is a great choice for this sauce. However, Pecorino Toscano (from Tuscany) or Pecorino Sardo (from Sardegna) are also excellent choices. Note that it is more difficult to make a super creamy sauce with 'aged' pecorino cheeses.

◆ ◆ ◆

PIATTO RECIPES

GARDEN PASTA

"Pasta all'Ortalana"

PREP TIME: 15 MINUTES **COOKING TIME:** 20 MINUTES | **SERVES:** 4

Pasta all'Ortolana, translated Garden Pasta, is the perfect way to use fresh summer veggies! There is no specific vegetable combination that is traditional, per se. However, eggplant, zucchini and a mix of peppers are common in many Italian Garden Pasta recipes. This dish is often prepared with some kind of fresh homemade pasta, such as Tuscan pici. However, you can simply choose your favorite pasta!

◆ ◆ ◆

INGREDIENTS

eggplant: 1/2 pound (220 g); about 1/2 large, diced

zucchini: 1 medium; diced
red pepper: 1/4 large; half minced and half thinly sliced
green pepper: 1/4 large; half minced and half thinly sliced
yellow pepper: 1/4 large; half minced and half thinly sliced
celery: 1/2 rib; minced
carrot: 1/2 carrot; minced
spring onion: 1/2; minced
olive oil: 5 tablespoons
white wine: 1/2 cup
butter: 2 tbsp
Parmigiano Reggiano: 3 oz (80 g); finely grated
pasta: 11 oz (320 g); fresh pici pasta or spaghetti or linguini

◆ ◆ ◆

STEP-BY-STEP

Or, watch the video recipe on our YouTube Cooking Channel!

Sauté The Vegetables

Cover the bottom of a skillet with olive oil. Sauté the minced onion, carrot and celery over medium heat until they are tender—about 5 minutes.

Add the diced eggplant, zucchini and pepper. Cook for about a minute, then add the white wine. Cover and cook covered until the vegetables are to your liking (more or less crunchy). Salt to taste. In the meantime…

Cook The Pasta

Cook the pasta you've selected to *al dente* according to package instructions. Be sure to save the hot pasta water. We need it to create the cheese sauce!

Finish With Pasta

Over low heat, add the cooked, drained pasta to the skillet with the vegetables along with a ladle of hot pasta water. Add the butter and stir to combine the ingredients. Then add the Parmigiano Reggiano cheese and continue stirring to create a creamy sauce that coats the pasta. Buon appetito!

WATCH IT

Or, watch the video recipe on our YouTube Cooking Channel!

◆ ◆ ◆

TIPS

Lighten it up!

We've recommended adding 2 tablespoons of butter to the Parmigiano Reggiano cheese in order to create a deliciously creamy sauce. To lighten up this dish, simply reduce the amount of butter you use and add a bit more hot pasta water.

Use Real Parmigiano

Use the real Parmigiano Reggiano cheese (not imitation cheeses or so-called parmesan).

When Presentation Matters

Does presentation matter? This dish will be delicious but less colorful if you cook the vegetables entirely in the skillet. To maintain the bright colors for a special occasion, you can quickly blanch the vegetables before adding them to the skillet.

Beware Bitter Eggplants

Avoid bitter eggplants! Look for 'Italian' eggplants or round bright purple eggplants rather than dark oblong eggplants. If you can't find these, use Japanese eggplants which tend to be sweeter and have a great taste.

◆ ◆ ◆

PIATTO RECIPES

PESTO PASTA WITH GREEN BEANS AND POTATOES

"Trofie al Pesto Genovese"

PREP TIME: 10 MINUTES **COOKING TIME:** 20 MINUTES | **SERVES:** 4

This is the quintessential use of Pesto Genovese among the locals in the city of Genoa, "Cinque Terre" and in the region of Liguria—where pesto was born! Pesto pasta is one of the freshest and tastiest summer dishes. You can enjoy it hot or as a cold pasta salad. This healthy and tasty recipe features authentic Pesto Genovese served with trofie pasta, potatoes and fresh green beans. Trofie is a handmade pasta typical of the region of Liguria in Italy. However, you can always substitute the trofie with fusilli, rigatoni or spaghetti.

◆ ◆ ◆

INGREDIENTS

fresh basil: 4.25 oz (120 g)
pecorino: 3.5 oz (100 g) freshly grated
Parmigiano Reggiano: 3.5 oz (100 g) freshly grated
garlic: 2 cloves, mashed by hand into a paste
coarse salt: pinch
pine nuts: 3.5 oz (100 g)
extra virgin olive oil: about 1/2 cup (100 g), or till you reach desired pesto consistency

yellow potatoes: 1/3 pound (150 g)
fresh green beans: 1/3 pound (150 g) ends removed
trofie pasta (or fusilli, rigatoni, spaghetti): 11 oz (320 g)

◆ ◆ ◆

STEP-BY-STEP

Or, watch the video recipe on our YouTube Cooking Channel!

Mash The Garlic And Salt

Mash the garlic cloves with a pinch of coarse salt until you have a paste. A mortar and pestle works great, but you can also use a garlic press. Do not use a blender or food processor for this. The heat from the blades will change the flavor of the garlic.

Make The Pesto

To the mortar or food processor bowl, add: the garlic paste, the grated pecorino, the grated Parmigiano Reggiano, the pine nuts and *half* of the basil.

Crush the ingredients until they are crumbly. Crush with the pestle using a circular motion. If you are using a blender or food processor, use quick, short pulses to blend the ingredients. This prevents the blade from getting hot and changing the taste of the fresh ingredients.

Add the rest of the basil. Slowly drizzle in several tablespoons of olive oil. Continue to blend using short, quick pulses with a food processor or blend with the pestle using a circular motion. Taste the pesto and add more salt if needed.

Drizzle in more olive oil, while continuing to blend. If you are using a food processor, it is now safe to use longer pulses to blend. Continue adding olive oil until you've reached the desired consistency. The final pesto should be a dense sauce. Don't exceed with the olive oil.

Blanch The Vegetables

Prepare a large bowl of ice water. This will be used for blanching the vegetables.

Peel the potatoes and cut them into bite-sized pieces. Bring a large pot of water to a boil. Add the chopped potatoes and fresh green beans to the boiling water. Cook until the potatoes are tender.

Transfer the drained potatoes and green beans immediately to the ice bath. When cool, drain the vegetables and set them aside. Save the hot water and use it to cook the pasta if you like!

Finish With Pasta

Cook the pasta according to package instructions for *al dente* pasta.

Drain the pasta. Mix half of the pesto and pasta together in a large bowl. Add the potatoes and green beans to the pasta. Add the rest of the pesto and mix combine.

Add a couple basil leaves for decoration and serve!

WATCH IT

Or, watch the video recipe on our YouTube Cooking Channel!

TIPS

Can't find trofie pasta?
Use fusilli, rigatoni or a long pasta like spaghetti or bucatini.

Serve hot... or cold!
This recipe is the perfect summertime fresh pasta salad. To turn this recipe into a cold pasta salad, blanch the pasta in an ice bath after you've cooked it. Assemble as above and serve.

Freshly grate the cheeses!
Freshness is the key to maximizing pesto's amazing flavor. Use freshly grated cheeses when at all possible.

Mash Garlic by Hand
Mash garlic into a paste by hand to avoid heating it with the food processor and changing the taste.

Using a food processor or immersion blender?
Use short pulses to made pesto with a food processor. This prevents the blade from getting too hot and changing the flavor of your fresh ingredients.

SUMMER PASTA COOKBOOK

NERANO SPAGHETTI

"Spaghetti alla Nerano"

PREP TIME: 10 MINUTES **COOKING TIME:** 30 MINUTES | **SERVES:** 4

This is a traditional dish from the city of Nerano, near Naples. The secret ingredient in this dish is fried zucchini, which gives the pasta an incredibly unique and earthy flavor. You'll love how the melted provolone and Parmigiano Reggiano cheeses hug the pasta to create a cheesy sauce. Absolutely irresistible!

◆ ◆ ◆

INGREDIENTS

provolone cheese: 5 oz (150 g); shredded
Parmigiano Reggiano: 1 oz (30 g); finely grated
zucchini: 1 1/2 pound (600 g); sliced thin with a mandolin

garlic: one clove, skin on
olive oil: 4 tbsp
fine salt: to taste
spaghetti: 11 oz (320 g)
oil for frying: safflower or your choice

◆ ◆ ◆

STEP-BY-STEP

Or, watch the video recipe on our YouTube Cooking Channel!

Fry The Zucchini

Slice the zucchini very thin (potato chip thin). Use a mandoline slicer to do this if you have one.

Fry the zucchini in batches at 300°F (150°C) until they become golden but not brown. This should take less than a minute! Flip the chips halfway through the frying.

Transfer the zucchini chips to an absorbent towel and lightly salt them. Don't rest the chips on top of each other.

Grate The Cheeses

Shred the provolone and finely grate the Parmigiano cheese.

Cook The Pasta

Cook the pasta for 3/4 of the time recommended for *al dente* pasta in the package instructions. In the meantime…

Sauté The Garlic And Zucchini

Cover the bottom of a large pan with olive oil. Over medium heat, sauté a clove of garlic 'shirt on' as they say in Italian! This just means to leave the papery skin on the garlic clove.

After the garlic has infused the oil with flavor (a couple of minutes), lower the heat. Then, add all but a handful of the fried zucchini chips to the infused oil and briefly stir. Keep the heat low to avoid burning the zucchini chips. Then, add 2 ladles of hot pasta water to the zucchini and oil.

The handful of fried zucchini that we set aside will be used to garnish the finished pasta!

Finish Cooking The Pasta

Transfer the spaghetti (cooked 3/4 of the way) to the pan with the zucchini. Add 2 more ladles of pasta water and finish cooking until spaghetti is cooked to *al dente*.

Add The Cheese

Remove the pan with the spaghetti from the heat. Add the provolone and Parmigiano cheeses along with another ladle of hot pasta water.

Mix the cheese with the pasta until it has melted and you've produced a thick and creamy pasta sauce! The cheese will be 'filante' or stringy.

Top the finished pasta with the fried zucchini you set aside and some leaves of fresh basil. The fresh basil is optional. Buon appetito!

WATCH IT

Or, watch the video recipe on our YouTube Cooking Channel!

♦ ♦ ♦

TIPS

Provolone Alternatives

The traditional cheese used for the *Nerano Spaghetti* is the *Provolone del Monaco*. This is a cheese from Naples, similar to caciocavallo cheese. It has a slight peppery flavor and melts wonderfully! Look for it in a specialty Italian or cheese shop. If you can't find it, substitute with your favorite provolone or caciocavallo cheese.

Frying Matters

A deep fryer is the ideal solution for making the zucchini chips. Deep fryers are cheap. They make tasks like frying chips easy because the deep fryer will maintain a steady temperature and fry the chips homogeneously. Deep fryers also do the job more quickly than pan frying. This means you are able to minimize the amount of oil that the chips absorb, creating healthier chips.

Don't want to fry? Buy the chips!

Some supermarkets do carry zucchini chips or dried zucchini slices. Use either of these if you don't want to fry the zucchini yourself.

Be sure to choose a product free of additional ingredients, like dehydrated garlic. Also avoid products high in salt. We want a product that will closely mimic the result you'd get if you fried those zucchini slices yourself!

◆ ◆ ◆

PIATTO RECIPES

SPAGHETTI WITH MUSSELS AND TOMATOES

"Spaghetti alle Cozze e Pomodorini"

PREP TIME: 10 MINUTES **COOKING TIME:** 10 MINUTES | **SERVES:** 4

Spaghetti with mussels and tomatoes is a traditional Italian seafood pasta recipe. It is popular in Italy during the Christmas holidays and anytime that fresh seafood can be found! Since mussels are more economical than many other types of shellfish and seafood, this is a recipe that need not be limited to special occasions.

◆ ◆ ◆

INGREDIENTS

mussels (rinsed and de-bearded): 3 pounds (1.5 kg)
spaghetti: 11 oz (320 g)
grape tomatoes: 14 oz (400 g)
garlic: 3 cloves (2 minced, 1 whole)
parsley: 2 handfuls (1 minced, 1 chopped)
red chili pepper: 1/2 or to taste
white wine: 1/4 cup (60 ml)
olive oil: 7+ tablespoons in total
salt and pepper: to taste

◆ ◆ ◆

STEP-BY-STEP

Or, watch the video recipe on our YouTube Cooking Channel!

Prepare The Mussels

Discard any mussels that are already open or have visible cracks. They are not safe to eat.

Use a paring knife to scrape any loose dirt or barnacles off of the mussels. Rinse the outside of the mussels.

You'll also want to remove the 'beard' from the mussels—the hairy looking tail that sticks out of the shell.

To remove the beard: Hold each mussel narrow side up. Grab the beard and pull down and away from the narrow side of the mussel until it pops off.

Steam The Mussels

Cover the bottom of a large pan or skillet with olive oil. Bring the skillet to medium heat. Then add one handful of parsley (roughly chopped) and one whole clove of garlic.

Sauté the garlic and herbs in the oil for about a minute. Then add the mussels and 1/4 cup (60 ml) of white wine to the skillet.

Cover and steam the mussels over medium heat until most of the shells have opened. This usually takes just a few minutes.

Discard any mussels that have not opened. Save a few steamed mussels for decoration. Remove the mussel meat from the rest of the shells and transfer them to a bowl.

Strain the broth that the mussels have produced while steaming. Add that broth to the mussel meat to prevent the mussels from drying out. Set the mussels aside.

Prepare The Sauce

Slice all of the grape tomatoes into quarters. Mince another handful of parsley with 2 cloves of garlic.

Cover the bottom of a large pan or skillet with olive oil. Bring the skillet to medium heat. Add the chili pepper, the minced garlic and the minced parsley to the hot oil.

After about 10 seconds, add the tomatoes as well. Give everything a stir. Then add 2 ladles of the mussel broth that you've saved.

Cover and cook the sauce over medium-low heat for about 5 minutes. Then add all of the mussel meat and another ladle of mussel broth. Continue to cook the sauce uncovered.

In the meantime...

Cook The Pasta

Add the spaghetti to boiling water and cook it for *half* of the time recommended on the package for *al dente* pasta. Do not salt the pasta water!

Finish With Pasta

Remove the chili pepper from the sauce and discard it.

Add the partially-cooked spaghetti to the skillet with the sauce along with 2 more ladles of hot pasta water. Mix to combine.

Finish cooking the spaghetti in the sauce over medium heat

until the pasta is cooked to *al dente*.

The sauce should thicken naturally from the starch coming from the spaghetti and hot pasta water.

At the end of the cooking time, add the mussels that you've saved for decoration back into the pasta to reheat them.

Top the finished pasta with a sprinkle of fresh minced parsley and serve!

WATCH IT

Or, watch the video recipe on our YouTube Cooking Channel!

◆ ◆ ◆

TIPS

How to Clean Mussels

Give them a rinse, then use a paring knife to scrape off any loose dirt, sand or barnacles. Mussels don't have much sand in the shell itself, so we don't need to pre-soak them as we might clams.

You will want to strain the mussel broth that this recipe produces before using it in the pasta sauce.

Salt the pasta water? No way!

Don't salt the pasta water! Seafood broth is naturally very salty. After the pasta is finished cooking, add salt to taste if needed.

◆ ◆ ◆

SUMMER PASTA COOKBOOK

SPAGHETTI CACIO AND PEPE

"Spaghetti Cacio e Pepe"

PREP TIME: 5 MINUTES **COOKING TIME:** 10 MINUTES | **SERVES:** 4

The perfect Cacio e Pepe is one of the most distinctive dishes that you will find in any Rome restaurant. This creamy sauce has just three ingredients: pecorino cheese ('cacio'), black pepper ('pepe') and pasta. The trick to achieving its unmatched flavor and creamy texture? Use quality ingredients and follow a few simple cooking tricks.

It's common to find the addition of heavy cream or another type of fat added to Cacio e Pepe made abroad. However, this is considered a big no-no in Italy. Even though the addition of cream makes it easier to create a creamy cheese sauce, Italians consider this an amateur's trick! Plus, cream changes the flavor of the dish.

Instead, the authentic creamy sauce in the Cacio e Pepe gets its texture from starchy pasta water mixed with finely grated pecorino cheese.

◆ ◆ ◆

INGREDIENTS

spaghetti: 11 oz (320 g) or pasta for 4
black pepper: 1-1.5 Tbsp, fresh ground (medium coarse)
Pecorino Romano cheese: 7 oz (200 g), finely grated

◆ ◆ ◆

STEP-BY-STEP

Or, watch the video recipe on our YouTube Cooking Channel!

Prepare The Ingredients

Finely grate the pecorino cheese. You may use a food processor to do this quickly, or just buy it already grated. It needs to be very finely grated, like a powder. Set aside.

Freshly grind the black pepper (1 Tbsp) using a medium-coarse setting. You can use a mortar and pestle if you prefer.

Toast The Black Pepper

Toast the pepper in a large skillet over medium heat just until fragrant—about 1 minute. Remove the skillet from the heat. Do not over toast! We don't want to create pepper gas.

Cook The Pasta

In a medium-large pot, bring water to boil. Add less water to the pot than you normally would when cooking pasta. For example, use 2 cups (500 ml) of water for every portion of pasta instead of 4 cups. Why? When the pasta cooks in less water, the water will have a higher concentration of starch coming from the pasta. This starchy pasta water will help us to create a creamy sauce!

Cook the pasta in the water for just *half* of the cooking time indicated on the package for *al dente* pasta—about 5 minutes.

While the pasta is cooking...

Simmer The Pepper

Add 2-3 ladles of the hot pasta water to the pan with the black pepper. Return the pan to the heat, and simmer the black pepper in the water for about 2 minutes.

Finish Cooking The Pasta

When the pasta is halfway cooked, transfer it to the skillet with the pepper-infused water, saving the hot pasta water!

Add another ladle of hot pasta water to the skillet with the pasta. Continue cooking the pasta for the rest of the cooking time required for *al dente* pasta, adding a ladle more of hot starchy pasta water to the skillet as needed.

In the meantime...

Make The Pecorino Sauce

Slowly drizzle in a ladle (100 ml) of the hot pasta water to the bowl with the finely grated pecorino cheese—whisking continuously!

Mix thoroughly until you've achieved a thick paste, similar in appearance to ricotta cheese.

The trick to making a creamy pecorino sauce and not a stringy mess, is to add the water when it is at a temperature of about 140° F (60° C). Any hotter, and the water will coagulate the cheese.

If you don't have a thermometer, drizzling the pasta water on the cheese a little at a time and whisking vigorously usually does the job.

Add The Cheese To The Pasta

Take the skillet with the cooked pasta off the heat.

Add the pecorino paste to the pasta and one ladle of hot pasta water. Stir the pecorino paste into the pasta quickly with a pair of tongs until the paste is distributed throughout the pasta

This will create a thick, creamy sauce (much like a béchamel). Add another ladle of hot water and stir again.

This process of creating a creamy texture with the aid of some fats is called 'mantecatura' in Italian.

If the pasta seems a bit too watery, don't worry. It will become denser after plating, as it continues to thicken.

Serve immediately. Buon appetito!

WATCH IT

Or, watch the video recipe on our YouTube Cooking Channel!

◆ ◆ ◆

TIPS

Choose Quality Ingredients

Use quality: semi-aged or fresh Pecorino Romano and freshly ground black pepper. With just two ingredients in this sauce, make sure those ingredients are bringing maximum flavor!

We'll say it again: Always use freshly ground black pepper in this dish to maximize the pepper flavor. Use a mortar and pestle to get a mix of fine and medium pepper grains, or use a medium-coarse setting on a pepper grinder.

Use a Food Processor to Grate Cheese

Save time by using a food processor to finely grate the cheese.

Avoid Clumps

To avoid clumpy cheese sauce, pay special attention to the quantity and temperature of the water used when making the pecorino sauce.

Though simple to make, many beginners end up with cheese sauce that contains unappetizing clumps. Since pecorino cheese melts at 140° F (60° C), adding water hotter than this to the cheese will usually produce a stringy, gummy sauce.

In this recipe, we avoid this error in two ways: adding the right quantity of pasta water at the right temperature (less than 140° F /60° C) to the pecorino cheese. You'll have perfect Cacio e Pepe every time!

◆ ◆ ◆

SUMMER PASTA COOKBOOK

PIATTO RECIPES

ABOUT THE AUTHOR

Piatto Recipes

PIATTO™ and PIATTO RECIPES™ cooking channels bring traditional Italian food recipes to your table with our easy, step-by-step video recipes. You'll find the best Italian recipes for breakfast, lunch, dinner and dessert. Always tested and always delicious!

Find our video recipes in English: youtube.com/piattorecipes

Find our video recipes in Italian: youtube.com/piatto

Printed in Great Britain
by Amazon

62486756R10038